POLISH *Classic* RECIPES

POLISH *Classic* RECIPES

LAURA & PETER ZERANSKI

PELICAN PUBLISHING COMPANY

GRETNA 2011

*The word "Pelican" and the depiction of a pelican are trademarks
of Pelican Publishing Company, Inc., and are registered in the
U.S. Patent and Trademark Office.*

ISBN 978-1-58980-961-1

Layout based on a design by Kit Wohl

Printed in China

Published by Pelican Publishing Company, Inc.
1000 Burmaster Street, Gretna, Louisiana 70053

We dedicate this book to the memory of Peter's Mother, Alina Żeranska, author of *The Art of Polish Cooking*, whose passion for Polish culture was the inspiration for this journey.

We also dedicate this book to the generations of young people who have not had the chance to create their own memories of Polish cuisine – yet!

Finally, we dedicate this book to Lucy Elisabeth Zeranski Ketchem, our granddaughter and newest member of our family, in the hope that she will continue the journey started by her Polish forbearers.

Laura and Peter Zeranski, Spring, 2011

CONTENTS

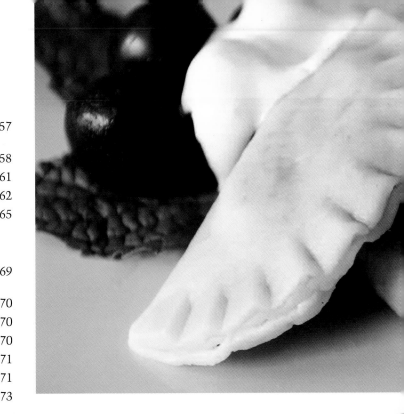

ierogi

weets and Pastries

INTRODUCTION

Welcome to a world of amazing flavors! Whether you are new to Polish cuisine, you want to rekindle the memories of meals enjoyed long ago, or you want to re-establish authentic Polish traditions of Christmas Eve, Easter and more, you're in for a treat!

The dishes in this book are but a small cross section of foods that have been lovingly handed down from mothers to daughters over many generations. These are many of the classic foods enjoyed at holidays and other festive occasions. These are foods many of us remember from our childhoods, and these are the foods that must be preserved for future generations, wherever they may settle around the world, beyond the borders of Poland.

Polish cuisine is very welcoming. There are clear, centuries-old historical influences from surrounding countries which resulted in Polish food having a character very much its own. It can be hearty and comforting on a windy and frosty winter night; it can be cool and refreshing under a blazing sun on a hot summer day. Polish cuisine can be elegant and refined on a Christmas Eve table set with fine china, elegant crystal, and heavy silverware. It can be simple and homey as prepared by generations of hard working grandmothers, who filled large pots with crunchy vegetables fresh from the garden and flavorful home-smoked meats from the farm. The aromas which are about to fill your kitchen will be wildly fragrant and intoxicating. Your guests will clamor to taste everything on the stove before sitting down to dine.

In today's world when many people think of Polish food, often what first comes to mind are pierogi, kielbasa, or cabbage rolls. But Polish cuisine actually goes far beyond these popular dishes. If you ever travel throughout Poland, regional influences will be evident. The food of the blue-collar working classes differs from the higher end dishes served in big city restaurants. The food of the Carpathian mountain region differs from the seafood dominated Baltic coast. This is no different from regional variations found in many other countries. Knowing that we had room in this book for only a few dishes, we chose them for their flavors and their authenticity to traditional dishes handed down through the generations. Throughout the selection process we kept in mind that it's about the food, it's about fabulous tastes, and it's about the smiles of friends and family around the table aimed your way when the meal is done.

Although this book is but a brief introduction to Polish cuisine, every recipe on these pages comes from a large body of dishes that we most remember as the heritage foods we grew up with. Each recipe has been extensively tested in our home kitchen, much to the delight of family and neighbors. Each dish is a "wow" combination of flavors. Each dish will look great on your table.

So as you get ready to turn the page, this book really comes down to just three key ideas: staying true to the roots of the dishes, presenting the recipes so that you can prepare them successfully, and seeing smiles around the table at the end of the meal.

Smacznego! (Polish for "bon appétit")

Laura and Peter Zeranski

APPETIZERS AND SALADS

Terrific meals start with terrific appetizers – special bites of tantalizing flavors meant to stimulate the appetite and prepare your guests for the next course. Whether called hors d'oeuvres, tapas, or antipasti, appetizers all serve the same purpose – to please and tease your palate.

Poles are very social. Food is an important part of entertaining and appetizers help set the stage for the evening. Some are best served from platters while guests are standing and milling in a typical cocktail party setting. An impressive selection could include one or two meats such as slices of ham or kielbasa, at least one fish such as herring or sardine, one or more patés from duck, pork or goose, a platter of artistically designed canapés, a selection of vegetables, mushrooms, and condiments such as beets with horseradish, mustard sauce, sour cream, and more.

Another way to serve appetizers is as a first course, after the guests are seated to dine. Heartier starters, such as Hunters Stew or Vegetable Salad, should be served in very small portions – leaving ample room for the delectable dishes to follow. In Poland these first courses have often been accompanied by icy shots of spirits such as Polish vodka - long considered among the best in the world, and served "purely as an aid to digestion."

Polish salads are quite different from the tossed greens we see today in restaurants or prepare at home, being more dependent on one or more flavored vegetables. Typical Polish flavor enhancers are chopped fresh dill, green onion, marjoram, or parsley. Polish dressings are simpler, often consisting of just sour cream mixed with either lemon juice or sugar, depending on whether a sweet or savory dressing is more appropriate.

Dill is a very important flavor element in Polish cuisine. It is best when fresh. If you have access to a grocery store or farmers market that sells fresh dill by the bunch, try to get it with the roots still on the stems. Wrap the roots (or stem-less ends) tightly in a wet paper towel, place the bunch in a plastic bag and store in the salad drawer in your refrigerator. When getting ready to use it, just rinse off the top to remove any sand, and slice just enough from the top as you need. Chop finely with a very sharp knife or herb chopper and sprinkle liberally. You can also store fresh dill in the freezer by wrapping individual small portions tightly in plastic wrap and placing the rolls into a freezer bag. They will keep for several months and can be used a portion at a time. It defrosts very quickly. Dried dill weed can be used as a substitute but it will not be as aromatic as the fresh dill. Substitute 1 teaspoon of dried dill for 1 tablespoon of the fresh.

CANAPÉS
Kanapki

How creative can you be? These multi-layer bites of goodness can be a great start to any dinner party or the perfect finger food to serve at cocktail parties. After World War II many Poles emigrated in search of a better life, often settling in communities with other Poles. Many were very social, often gathering on Saturday evenings to eat and perhaps dance to sultry pre-war romantic ballads. Most of these gatherings featured the dishes they grew up with, perhaps started with platters of canapés – little rounds of rye or pumpernickel artfully layered with components such as: cheeses spreads, green and black olives, small pieces of sardine, slices of herring or anchovy, tiny cubes of cheese, thin slices of kielbasa, and more. It was all about the ingredients, the balance of flavors, and the presentation.

Rye bread, cut in small rounds, triangles or squares
French baguette, sliced in thin rounds
Variety of cold meats, cheese and vegetables

Spread the bread with butter, or one of the following spreads:

Mustard Butter
1/2 cup softened butter
1/2 cup seeded mustard

Mix the butter with the mustard until creamy.

Herb Butter
1/2 cup softened butter
1 tablespoon herb, such as dill, parsley or chives, or several combined

Mix the butter with the herbs.

Horseradish Butter
1/2 cup softened butter
1 tablespoon horseradish, more or less to taste

Mix the butter with the horseradish.

Top the buttered bread rounds with layers of meat, cheese, vegetables, and dressings of your choice.

TIP: *Spreads work well as the bottom layer; a firm ingredient such as slice of kielbasa or hard boiled egg provide a solid middle foundation; top with the smaller and more colorful elements such as a slice of green olive with pimiento.*

Some suggested combinations are:

- Sardines, swiss cheese, tomato
- Ham, dill pickle, mustard
- Kielbasa, Beets with Horseradish *(page 49)*
- Smoked salmon, lettuce, mayonnaise
- Salami, cheese, dill pickle slice
- Hard boiled egg slice, mayonnaise, radish
- Herring, egg, tomato
- Paté, vegetable salad, green olive

YEAST FINGERS
Drożdżowe Paluszki

These are tasty little "fingers" that go very well with soups or beverages. Putting a little caraway or poppy seed on top gives them a savory note that balances very well with heartier soups such as Polish Sour Soup or Dill Pickle Soup. If you are feeling adventuresome, you could mix the caraway with a little bit of your favorite herb, or experiment with the dough by forming it into different shapes, adding cheese to the dough, or using a sweet topping.

YIELDS 35 to 40

1 cup butter
4 1/2 cups flour, sifted
4 1/2 teaspoons yeast
2 teaspoons sugar
1 teaspoon salt
2 eggs
2 egg yolks
1/4 cup warm milk
1/4 cup sour cream
1 egg beaten
Caraway seeds, poppy seeds, coarse salt for topping

Cut the butter into the flour and rub in with fingertips. Mix yeast with sugar and add to warm milk. Add to the butter and flour mixture. Add salt, eggs, egg yolks and sour cream. Knead the dough for a few minutes until dough pulls away from the sides of the bowl and is smooth and elastic. It will be slightly sticky.

Note: Dough can also be made using a mixer with dough hook attachment, or a food processor.

Divide the dough into 1 inch balls and form into long thin rolls about 6 inches each. Place on greased cookie sheet and let rise in your oven which has been set on Low. When doubled in size, brush the dough fingers with beaten egg and sprinkle with seeds or coarse salt. Bake in a 375 degree oven for 12-15 minutes. Remove from cookie sheet immediately.

Serve with other appetizers or soups.

CREPES WITH SAUERKRAUT AND MUSHROOMS
Naleśniki z Kapustą i Grzybami

When Laura prepares Christmas Eve supper *(Wigilia)*, following the traditions that Peter grew up with, which are the same traditions that his parents and their parents grew up with, these stuffed crepes are everybody's favorite part of the meal. They go really well with a cup of Classic Beet Soup *(page 29)* which is a characteristic way to serve them. The blend of savory sauerkraut mixed with earthy mushrooms in an amazing combination. This dish is an ideal starter, whether for Christmas Eve or any other festive meal.

YIELDS 8 to 10 croquets

CREPES

1 cup milk	1 cup flour	1/2 teaspoon salt
2 eggs	1/2 cup water	3 tablespoons vegetable oil

Mix the milk with the eggs, flour, water and salt in a blender or hand mixer at low speed. Heat a small non-stick skillet which measures 6 to 7 inches across the base (crepe pans are great) and brush or lightly spray the bottom with cooking oil. Pour a small amount of batter into the medium hot skillet. (For a 6 inch pan use a just under 1/3 cup of batter per crepe.) Immediately start swirling the pan around so the batter will evenly cover the bottom and put back on the burner. When the crepe becomes firm on top, maybe 45 to 60 seconds, and just starts to lightly brown on the bottom, turn it over and cook the other side for another 15 seconds or so. Remove the crepe from the pan and stack on a plate with a sheet of wax paper between crepes to prevent sticking. Continue this process until all the batter is used – you should get 8 to 10 crepes from one batch.

FILLING

1/2 pound sauerkraut	4 ounces mushrooms, sliced	1 egg beaten
2 tablespoons butter or	salt and pepper	1/2 cup bread crumbs
rendered bacon fat	1 hard boiled egg, chopped	3 tablespoons butter
1 onion, chopped	2 tablespoons sour cream	

Rinse the sauerkraut thoroughly in a colander. Squeeze the sauerkraut to remove the excess water. Place the sauerkraut in a small amount of boiling water. Cook for 20 minutes and drain. Heat the butter or bacon fat in a skillet, add the onions and fry until golden. Add the mushrooms and fry an additional 3 minutes. Add the sauerkraut and fry until golden. Salt and pepper to taste. Remove from the heat and add the egg and sour cream. Mix well.

Spoon a small amount of the filling into the center of a crepe. Fold the crepe in envelope fashion to completely encase the filling. Roll the stuffed crepe in egg and then in bread crumbs. Gently fry crepes in butter until golden on both sides. Serve either hot or warm.

Peter is the crepe maker; here are his hints after 40 years of practice: First try a test batch or two to perfect the technique (spread a little jam on the rejects for a great snack). Once the batter starts to firm up in the pan, gently shake it to just loosen the crepe. Now you can peek at the bottom so check the browning, plus it will be easier to slide your spatula underneath. If the batter starts to bubble as soon as you pour it into the pan, turn down the heat a bit. The pan will get hotter after several crepes, so let it cool down periodically. Bubbly crepes will not have a consistent thickness and tend to turn brown faster. To turn the crepe use the widest and thinnest spatula you have. If the crepe is loose from the pan, you can slide the spatula underneath (quickly) and flip. After they have cooled, test your filling/folding skill just with left-over sauerkraut, saving the best filling for the best crepes. If the crepe is too thin it may tear when folded around the filling. Small tears, up to ¼ inch, should hold up but the filling will fall out if the tears are larger. If you have torn up several practice crepes, try using more batter – 1/3 cup batter should be enough for a pan that measures 6 inches across the bottom.

RED CABBAGE WITH APPLES
Czerwona Kapusta z Jabłkami

This salad is strikingly different than most salads that are based on greens, both in taste and its bright, inviting appearance. Cabbage is a wonderfully nutritious and versatile vegetable, enjoyed throughout the world in a number of colorful varieties. Red cabbage pairs very well with rich flavors such as sage, thyme, caraway, dill, fennel, horseradish, apples, onions, chestnuts, juniper berries, and sour cream. The freshness and light tang of this salad make it a superb pairing with heavier meats such as beef, duck or venison. Any available variety of sweet apple will work fine. Laura used Gala apples for testing the recipe.

SERVES 6 to 8

1 small head of red cabbage, shredded
salt
2 large apples, peeled and shredded
Juice of 2 lemons
4 tablespoons sugar

Cook the shredded cabbage in salted boiling water for 5 to 7 minutes. Drain and cool. Combine the lemon juice and sugar to make dressing. Toss cabbage and apples with the dressing. Refrigerate for 1 hour before serving.

Cabbage seems to be one of those wonder foods that has many amazingly healthy properties. It is said that cabbage is rich in Vitamin A, B, C and D, detoxifying phyto-nutrients, iodine, antioxidants, and other healthy nutrients. Its health benefits have been broadly touted for all sorts of conditions, ranging from lowering the incidence of certain cancers, treating fungus infections, building muscle, boosting energy metabolism, burning fat, preventing ulcers, and much more. While it is not the purpose of this book to promote medical cures for anything whatsoever, and the authors are certainly not qualified to do that, there is so much literature on the internet about the benefits of eating cabbage. Early medicine practices relied heavily on herbs, berries and natural ingredients, so it is quite probable that classic cabbage recipes such as this salad and the other recipes in this book, were promoted for their healthy properties as well as for their good taste.

Cucumber Salad
Mizeria

This is a very simple dish that takes only minutes to prepare. Its refreshing flavors make it a wonderful side on a hot summer day. Legend has it that *Mizeria* (which means "misery" in Polish) was a favorite of Queen Bona Sforza (1494-1557), Queen of Poland and Grand Duchess of Lithuania. The story goes that this dish was so named because she recalled the flavors from her childhood in Italy and was "in misery," yearning to taste those flavors again. But when you serve this dish, no one will be "in misery" for sure.

SERVES 4 to 6

1 large cucumber (peeled if desired)
1/2 teaspoon salt
Pepper to taste
1/2 cup sour cream
1 teaspoon sugar
2 1/4 teaspoons lemon juice (or more to taste)
1 tablespoon chopped dill leaves

Thinly slice the cucumbers. Sprinkle slices with salt and let stand for a few minutes while the water releases. Lightly press excess water from cucumbers. Sprinkle slices with pepper. Arrange them on a platter or in a shallow bowl.

Mix the sour cream, sugar and lemon juice to make the dressing.

Spread the dressing over the cucumber slices. Generously sprinkle the dill over the salad. Chill well before serving.

VEGETABLE SALAD
Sałatka Jarzynowa

This salad is very easy to make. It looks so colorful on the table and on your plate. It's full of fresh, bright garden flavors and pairs well with all the important dishes served at Christmas, Easter and other important holidays. You can prepare this well ahead, in fact the flavors are better after spending the night in the refrigerator. This type of salad with diced vegetables bound in mayonnaise is found in many ethnic cuisines. It differs only in the use of local flavorings and ingredients – the Polish version does not spare the dill. Make a lot and everyone will love you for it.

SERVES 12 to 14

4 cups cooked, diced potatoes
4 cups frozen mixed vegetables, cooked and drained
2 cups frozen peas, cooked and drained
3 large dill pickles, diced (optional)
1/2 cup chopped green onion
2 tablespoons dill leaves chopped
Salt and pepper
3/4 cup mayonnaise
3/4 cup sour cream
2 tablespoons prepared yellow mustard
2 hard boiled eggs, chopped or sliced

Mix the potatoes with the vegetables, pickles, onions and dill. Season with salt and pepper.

Mix mayonnaise with sour cream and mustard. Combine dressing and vegetable mixture.

Chill thoroughly. Arrange salad in a pretty bowl. Sprinkle top with the chopped or sliced egg. A few slices of radish and sprigs of dill will add a nice touch of color.

MARINATED BEET SALAD
Sałatka z Buraków

Here's an excellent use for the beets left over after making Classic Beet Soup *(page 29)*. Fresh beets are wonderfully light, aromatic, and surprisingly flavorful. Some people turn up their noses at beets but those opinions have usually been influenced by canned, pickled beets which are much stronger tasting. Poles have always loved beets, as evidenced by their influence on Polish cuisine. This salad has remained very popular for generations, even among the "doubters."

SERVES 6

3 cups cooked beets, cut in 1/4 inch julienne
1 cup of finely sliced green onion
2/3 cup currants
2 tablespoons olive oil
3 tablespoons red wine vinegar
salt and pepper to taste
1 bunch leaf lettuce (optional)
green onion for garnish

Combine beets, onion and currants. Whisk the oil and vinegar and toss with beet mixture. If desired, arrange on lettuce leaves to serve. Garnish with finely sliced green onion.

Peter's parents emigrated from Poland to Canada shortly after World War II. In those days, the law required all male immigrants to have a job guaranteed by an official sponsor. Peter's Dad and his brother-in-law, Mike Domecki, began their Canadian lives pulling beet roots on a farm near Winnipeg, Ontario. They were both university-trained engineers, and after a time were given other work that was less back-breaking. However, during their time in the fields they had pulled so many beet roots, and ate so many beets dishes provided by their beet-farmer boss, that Peter's Dad could not enjoy beets for the rest of his days, even though he used to love them growing up in Poland.

SOUPS AND SOUP GARNISHES

Soups have been a cornerstone of traditional Polish cuisine for a very long time. Culinary historians have actually traced the roots of one iconic Polish soup to 997 AD when it was known as Fermented Barley Flour Soup. In the early 16th century, Italian Princess Bona Sforza, Queen of Poland in 1518, had a huge influence on Polish cuisine by introducing salads, soup greens and various soup vegetables. As Polish cuisine continued to evolve over many generations of Polish cooks, soups became more refined, more varied, and a major component of many meals – from light lunches, hearty suppers, to sweet and satisfying endings.

Winters are often long and cold in Poland and soups have always been the perfect comfort food for warming up hard working bodies and souls. Polish soups can be hearty and substantial, thick with vegetables and meats, or more refined, delicate, and clear, flavored with herbs and vegetable stocks – enjoyed best when sipped from a gracious, fine china cup.

The most traditional Polish soups have remained unchanged through history. The tastiest classic examples find their roots in the rich earth, broad plains, and tall, proud forests, which offered an abundance of potatoes, pickles, beets and mushrooms, as well as grains such as barley and lentils. In this chapter you will find a splendid cross section of essential Polish flavors, from the very familiar and classic aromas of earthy dried mushrooms, to the wonderfully aromatic notes of marjoram, and dill – a favorite herb of eastern European cuisines. Finally, we end with sweet, refreshing and amazingly flavorful summer fruit soups made from ripe strawberries, raspberries, or blueberries.

Classic Beet Soup
Barszcz

Barszcz is one of Poland's most iconic and popular soups – a proud national treasure. Ukrainians, Russians and Poles have claimed and debated its origin for millennia. There are literally hundreds of versions, with each region, town, and village having its own favorite. But that doesn't really matter because it's the goodness that is most important. The flavor of *Barszcz* is best when prepared with fresh beets and a good-quality broth. *Barszcz* can vary in consistency. Lighter, clear versions are often served in an elegant china cup. Heartier versions may include vegetables, beans or meats and eaten with just a hunk of bread or boiled potato. This particular recipe is a more up-scale, lighter version and is often enjoyed with appetizers such as Crepes *(page 17)* at *Wigilia*, the traditional Christmas Eve supper.

SERVES 6

6 medium beets
6 cups beef broth
1 tablespoon lemon juice
1 teaspoon sugar
1/4 teaspoon pepper
1/8 teaspoon garlic powder
Salt to taste
1/2 cup red wine

Wash and bake the beets in a 350 degree oven for 30 minutes. Peel and coarsely grate the beets. Add the beets to the broth and simmer for 5 minutes. Strain the beets from the broth. To the broth, add the seasonings and the wine.

Soup may be served as is, or with Mushroom Pockets, *Uszka*, *(page 30)*.

Save the cooked beets for another use such as Marinated Beet Salad *(page 25)*.

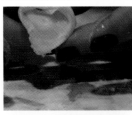

(recipe continued from right)
2 inch squares. Place a small amount of filling in the center of each square. Brush the edges of the square lightly with beaten egg. Fold the square diagonally to form a triangle. Seal the edges of the triangle with your fingers. Lift the 2 long corners of the triangle up and press the points together to seal.

In a large pot of well salted boiling water, cook the mushroom pockets for 3 to 4 minutes after they have floated to the top.

TIP: *At first, the dumplings may stick to the bottom of the pot. Give them a gentle nudge with spatula or spoon and they will pop to the top.*

Remove pockets from the water and drain. Place a few pockets in each bowl of soup as a garnish, and serve immediately.

MUSHROOM POCKETS FOR BARSZCZ
Uszka do Barszczu

These little bites of goodness are an important part of a traditional Christmas Eve menu. They are best served with Classic Beet Soup *(page 29)*. Italians have their little tortellini and Poles have *Uszka*. Both are quite similar in size and shape.

YIELDS 20 to 24 Pockets

FILLING

4 ounces mushrooms, finely chopped
2 tablespoons butter
1 small onion, finely chopped
4 tablespoons fresh breadcrumbs
2 tablespoons parsley, finely chopped
1 large beaten egg
salt and pepper

Melt butter in a large skillet. Add the onion and sauté until translucent, about 5 minutes.

Add the chopped mushrooms to the onions and cook an additional 10 minutes, or until the liquid has evaporated and the mixture starts to sizzle.

Put the onion and mushroom mix in a large bowl. Add the breadcrumbs, parsley and the beaten egg. Season with salt and pepper. Mix everything together to form a firm paste. Allow the paste to cool slightly before filling the pockets. The filling will keep in the refrigerator for 24 hours.

DOUGH

1 egg
1/3 cup milk
1/8 teaspoon salt
1 cup flour
1 egg for sealing, beaten with 1 tablespoon water

Whisk together the first egg, milk and salt. Stir in half of the flour until flour is incorporated, then add the other half and continue to stir. After the mixture comes together into a thick sticky dough, place the dough on a floured surface. Using additional flour knead the dough until it is smooth, supple and soft – but not sticky. Form the dough into a ball, wrap it in plastic wrap or cover with a bowl to keep it from being exposed to air. Let it rest for 15 minutes.

Take half of the dough and on a floured surface roll it out as thin as possible. It should be almost see-through, approximately 1/8 inch. Cut the dough into 1 1/2 or
(recipe continued at left)

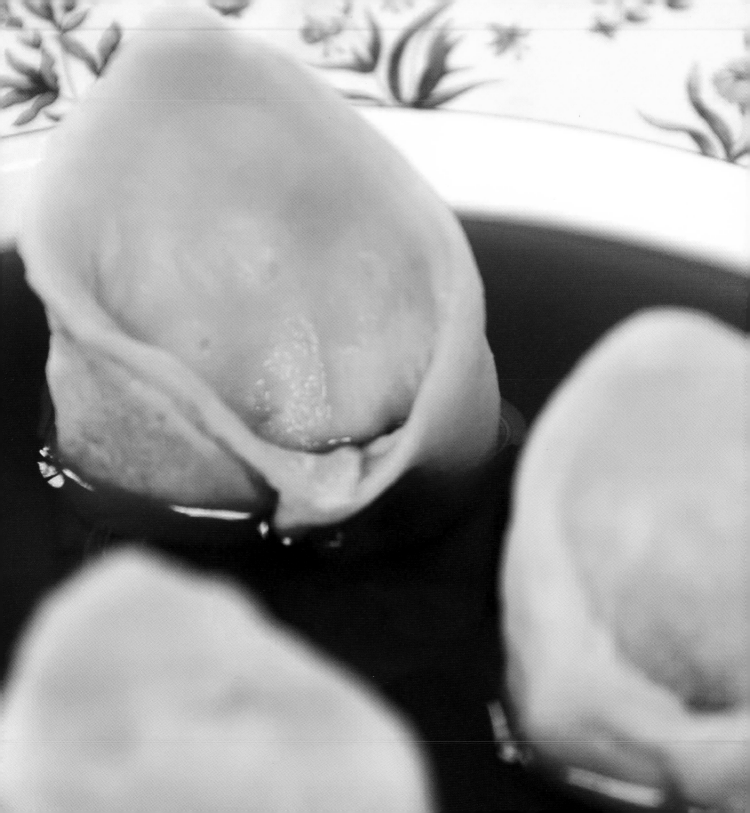

Cool Summer Barszcz
Chłodnik

This summer soup is one of those "go-to" recipes to pull out as a sure-fire hit, even for friends who have not yet discovered the delicious charm of beets. The Polish name of this soup is a modification from the Polish word for "cool." While several versions of Barszcz originated throughout Eastern Europe, many acknowledge that Cool Summer Barszcz is unique to Poland. This soup has been around for centuries and is among the world's best as a summer cooler. Full of garden flavors and vegetable crunch, it's immensely refreshing as the most perfect lunch or light supper. Laura and Peter serve it just by itself or with a hunk of fresh aromatic rye bread and smear of sweet butter. When their guests first see it, the typical reaction is: "wow, it looks so pretty!" Then after a few spoonfuls - "wow, I never knew beets could be so good!"

SERVES 10

2 cups fresh beets, peeled and cut in 1/4 inch julienne
1 cup water
1/4 cup beet stems, coarsely chopped
1 cup beet leaves, coarsely chopped
1 teaspoon red wine vinegar
4 cups beef broth
2 tablespoons flour
1/4 cup cold water
2 hard boiled eggs, sliced

1 small cucumber, peeled and sliced
1 cup sliced roast pork or veal
8 large shrimp, cooked, peeled, and diced (Optional)
1/8 teaspoon garlic powder
1 teaspoon sugar
1 tablespoon lemon juice
1 cup sour cream
1 tablespoon chopped dill
1 tablespoon chopped green onion

Simmer the beets, leaves and stems in 1 cup of water and vinegar for 20 to 25 minutes, until the beets are completely soft and tender. Add the beef broth and simmer 5 minutes longer.

Mix the flour into 1/4 cup water, add to the beet mixture and stir. Cook for an additional 3 to 5 minutes. Cool completely. Add the rest of the ingredients and chill for several hours. Serve cold.

Time Saver Version
2 cups canned beets, drained and cut in 1/4 inch julienne
1/4 cup beet juice
1 cup chopped kale or swiss chard
1 teaspoon red wine vinegar
4 cups beef broth

Simmer the beets, stems and leaves in 1/4 cup of beet juice and the vinegar for 3 to 5 minutes. Add the beef broth and simmer 5 minutes longer.

From this point, pull remaining ingredients from above, starting with the 2 tablespoons of flour, and continue the recipe from the point of mixing the flour into 1/4 cup of water.

TIP: For a truly stunning presentation, garnish the soup with a few whole shrimp, slices of hard boiled egg, and sprinkles of dill. While not everyone appreciates a shrimp with its head on, the visual effect is dramatic. Laura keeps a scrapbook of memorable dishes, and this soup is worth photographing and saving.

POLISH SOUR SOUP
Żurek

If *Barszcz* is claimed by many as the national soup of Poland, then this delicacy is a very close second. Unlike *Barszcz*, whose roots are claimed by several Eastern European nations, many Poles believe that this soup's origins are undeniably Polish. A distinctive feature is its somewhat sour flavor, though by no means unpleasant. The name comes from the soup starter, made of rye flour and water which lightly ferments or "sours" over a few days. Though this soup is seen in many regional and personal interpretations, a typical bowl will include at least one boiled egg and a healthy portion of sliced kielbasa. The white version is more often available around Christmas time, and is preferred if you can get it. Toss in some potato chunks, a few vegetables and the flavorings. Let it all simmer for a while and you're essentially done. That's why this classic recipe is sometimes called "yesterday's menu soup."

Note: the first time Laura made this starter, it was Peter's job to stir. Every time he uncovered the bowl, he would wrinkle his nose at the whiff of fermenting rye. But when the soup was finished, he declared it was as good as any version he had eaten in Poland.

SERVES 6 to 8

RYE STARTER
Start this mixture 5 to 6 days before making the soup.
1/2 cup rye flour
4 cups warm water

Stir flour and water together in a ceramic bowl or container. Cover the container with a cloth and set it in a warm spot. Stir gently once a day. The natural fermentation will create a slight sour smell in the bowl. After 5 days, stir one last time and strain the mixture, before adding to the soup.

SOUP

6 cups of vegetable broth	8 slices of bacon, diced	1/2 teaspoon marjoram
2 bay leaves	10 mushrooms, sliced	1 cup sour cream (optional)
1 pound potatoes, diced	2 cups rye starter	6 hard boiled eggs
1/2 pound smoked Polish sausage (kielbasa), sliced	1/2 teaspoon salt	
	1/4 teaspoon pepper	

Bring broth to a boil, add the bay leaves and simmer while preparing other ingredients.

In a skillet, partially cook the bacon until almost crisp. Add the onion and sausage and cook until the onions are golden. Add the mushrooms and cook for another 3 to 5 minutes until the mixture is lightly browned.

Add the bacon, onion, sausage, and mushroom mix to the vegetable broth. Add the potatoes. Pour in the rye starter and stir well. Season with salt, pepper and marjoram. Simmer uncovered 20 minutes.

(recipe continued at right)

(recipe continued from left)
Add the sour cream to thicken the soup, if desired.

To serve, first cut the eggs in quarters, length wise, and place four quarters in each soup bowl. Pour the soup gently around the egg.

CHRISTMAS DRIED MUSHROOM SOUP
Wigilijna Zupa z Suszonych Grzybów

As far back as the 18th century, mushrooms have been considered a food of all the people. City folks and country folks alike have always enjoyed vast varieties of mushrooms. Hearty mushroom soups were often a mainstay of meatless Fridays and other Catholic observances. Today mushroom soup is often served as a starter for traditional Christmas Eve supper (*Wigilia*). Many international cuisines feature their own mushroom soups and many are also based on dried mushrooms. But if you have ever tasted wild mushrooms that were harvested from Polish forests, you know that these have a flavor and intensity that is unique in the world. Since they don't stay fresh long enough for export, using dried mushrooms is the next best thing. This soup is best if you can find dried Polish mushrooms in a deli or specialty store. And if you can't decide whether to serve Christmas Dried Mushroom Soup or Classic Beet Soup at your next traditional Christmas Eve supper, the solution is easy – just serve both.

SERVES 4 to 6

2 cups dried mushrooms	1/4 teaspoon white pepper
2 1/2 cups water	1 tablespoon flour
6 cups water	2 tablespoon butter
1 large onion, diced	3 tablespoons of cold water
1 large shallot, diced	1 tablespoon vinegar
1 leek, thinly sliced	1/2 cup sour cream
2 carrots	1 tablespoon butter
3 stalks of celery with leaves	1 tablespoon chopped fresh dill
3/4 teaspoon salt	leaves, or 1 teaspoon dried

Soak the dried mushrooms in 2½ cups of water for 2 hours. Strain the mushrooms through a fine strainer or cheese cloth to remove any sand, reserving the liquid for the soup. Chop the mushroom finely. Put the mushrooms, reserved mushroom liquid and the 6 cups of water in a large soup pot. Add the onion, shallot and leeks. Bring the mixture to a boil, cover and simmer for 30 minutes.

Add the carrots and celery. Season the soup with salt and pepper, cover and simmer for 30 more minutes. Remove the carrots and celery from the soup, press lightly over the pot to extract all the juices, and discard. Strain the mushrooms, onion, shallots and leeks from the soup and finely chop. Return the chopped mix to the soup broth.

In a sauté pan, melt the butter and add the flour to make a roux. Heat for 3 to 5 minutes while constantly stirring until it turns to a rich amber color. Add 3 tablespoons of cold water and continue stirring until the mixture is thickened and smooth. Add the roux to the soup. Add the vinegar. Adjust the seasonings. Mix in the sour cream, butter and dill. Serve hot.

Irka's Time Saver Version

1 cup dried mushrooms
2 cups hot water
1 can good quality beef consommé
1 can good quality beef broth
1 onion
dash of white pepper

Soak the dried mushrooms in the hot water for 2 hours or more. Strain the mushrooms through a fine strainer or cheese cloth to remove any sand. Reserve the mushroom liquid. Chop the mushrooms.

Combine the consommé, beef broth and onion in a soup pot and bring to a boil. Remove the onion from the broth and discard. Add the mushrooms and the reserved liquid to the broth. Add the white pepper.

CHILLED FRUIT SOUP
Chłodnik Owocowy

Poles certainly love their soups, and cool summer fruit soups are no exception. Many versions, such as the strawberry version presented here, can be eaten hot or cold. These days fruit soups are often thought of as gourmet food, but actually they have their roots with Polish farmers who ate them cold as a thirst-quenching lunch on a hot summer day. Serve with golden croutons for some crunch.

SERVES 4

1 quart strawberries or raspberries
4 cups buttermilk
2/3 cup sour cream
1/2 cup sugar

Blend berries with 1 cup of the buttermilk in blender or using an immersion blender. Wisk the remaining 3 cups of buttermilk with the sour cream and the sugar, and add to the berry mixture. Chill thoroughly. Serve with croutons.

CROUTONS

4 slices of white bread cut in small cubes
2 tablespoons of butter, melted

Toss the bread cubes in the melted butter until all cubes are evenly coated. Lay the cubes on a single layer on a baking sheet. Place in the oven under the broiler. Broil until all cubes are golden brown, tossing occasionally to ensure even browning on all sides.

DILL PICKLE SOUP
Zupa Ogórkowa

This is one of those uniquely special soups which are particularly memorable. Don't let the name scare you away – much of the pungent pickle flavor cooks off, leaving an aromatic, flavorful broth that does not overpower. Laura and Peter suggest that if you have access to a Polish or Russian deli, try making this soup with dill pickles imported from Poland. They are a little sweeter than American varieties. Serve with a crusty hunk of seeded rye bread and sweet butter.

SERVES 6 to 8

6 cups beef broth
2 tablespoon flour
1 cup milk
1 egg yolk
2 tablespoon soft butter
4 large dill pickles, shredded
2/3 cup dill pickle liquid
2 1/2 cups boiled, cubed potatoes
2 carrots sliced
1/2 teaspoon parsley, chopped
1/2 teaspoon dill, chopped
3 tablespoons sour cream (optional)

Bring the broth to a boil. Mix the flour with the milk and add to the broth. Bring mix to a boil. Remove from the heat.

Mix the egg yolk with the butter and add to broth mixture. Add the pickles, pickle liquid, potatoes, and carrot. Heat but do not boil. Add the sour cream if desired. Garnish with parsley and dill.

This soup lends itself particularly well to being served in a bread bowl of dark rye or hearty pumpernickel.

ENTRÉES
AND SIDE DISHES

The entrée is the centerpiece of the meal – the hero that all supporting culinary characters must honor. Whether a tender cut of roast, flaky portion of fish, or vegetarian meal, the entrée is the main attraction.

Poles are traditionally meat eaters – especially pork, beef, and chicken. Pork has always been a special favorite, prepared as roasts, chops, cutlets, and as the main ingredient of kielbasa. Wild boar, duck, and other game meats are viewed as delicacies, but they are not so much in the mainstream.

ON KIELBASA – Spaniards have chorizo, Italians have salami, Germans have bratwurst, Americans have the hotdog, and the British have a whole array of bangers. Polish sausage, known the world over as kielbasa, comes in as many varieties as there are kielbasa makers, but in general, the more common varieties differ only by the amounts of fat, garlic, and spices combined with the mix. For Laura and Peter's taste, kielbasa purchased at a Polish or Russian deli, often made in New York or Chicago, is far superior to mass-produced varieties sold in large grocery stores. It can be as authentic as any kielbasa they've tasted in Poland. The good ones are leaner and the flavors are definitely more pronounced. In a deli, tasting is often encouraged and Laura and Peter always note how some taste – more or less garlicky, more or less herby, and more or less smoky. If you can visit such a deli, popular varieties that are a good bet include Wiejska (country style), Krakowska (Krakow style), or Podwawelska (a style named for the famous Wawel Castle in Krakow). One thing is for sure, better qualities of kielbasa will make a huge difference in how these dishes taste.

This chapter shares just a few of Laura and Peter's favorite classic dishes. These are the ones they have prepared over and over again for regular mid-week meals when Peter gets an occasional craving for flavors he grew up with, as well as for holidays and social events. That's the beauty and flexibility of these dishes – they can satisfy anyone's cravings for comfort food at the kitchen table, plus they can truly delight family and honored guests at a more festive meal in the formal dining room, at an elegant table set with your finest china, Grandmother's heirloom silverware, and delicate crystal goblets.

HUNTER'S STEW
Bigos Myśliwski

This is a traditional stew native to Poles and Lithuanians, and is considered by many to be one of Poland's true national dishes. Its composition can vary from region to region, village to village, and restaurant to restaurant. This is hearty comfort food at its best. Poles often serve it with crusty rye bread or boiled potatoes on the side (of course, well lubricated with chopped dill and melted butter). For a truly authentic experience, a shot of ice-cold Polish vodka goes down very smoothly. Laura's little kitchen secret is that *Bigos* is a great way to use up leftover meats. She often freezes extra pieces of pork loin or beef roast to save for the next *Bigos*. In fact, sometimes she will make an extra pork chop just to put away for later. Some of Laura and Peter's best dinner parties have been around a big bowl of *Bigos*, washed down with glasses of hearty red wine.

SERVES 5 to 6

1/4 cup dried mushrooms
1/2 cup water
2 pounds sauerkraut
1 large apple, peeled, cored and sliced
2 1/2 cups canned tomatoes
5 peppercorns
1 bay leaf
1 cup fully cooked Polish sausage, sliced and quartered
1 cup leftover meat (pork, beef, veal) chopped in 1 inch pieces
1 cup coarsely chopped bacon, pre-cooked to render fat

Soak the dried mushrooms in the water for 2 hours. Place the mushrooms and water in a small pan. Bring to a boil and simmer for 30 minutes. Drain the mushrooms reserving the liquid. Chop the mushrooms into rough pieces.

Wash the sauerkraut thoroughly and squeeze out the water. Put the sauerkraut in a large pot. Add the mushrooms and the reserved liquid. Add the apples, tomatoes, peppercorns and bay leaf. Break up the tomatoes into small pieces. Cover and simmer for 1 hour and 15 minutes, stirring occasionally.

Add the meat and bacon. Cover and simmer 1 hour longer, stirring occasionally.

This dish tastes much better when reheated the next day.

TIP: *There are no strict recipe rules for making an amazing Hunter's Stew. The apple, tomatoes, and proportions of meats to sauerkraut can be easily varied to suit anyone's taste. Dried mushrooms are key to this particular version and if you can get the ones imported from Poland, the earthy flavors will be more intense. Pork and sausage are an excellent combination of meats but almost anything goes.*

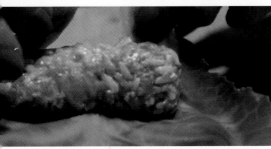

CABBAGE ROLLS
Gołąbki

Cabbage comes back to your kitchen here as leaves of the basic green variety are used to envelope a delightfully tasty mix of beef, pork, and rice. Legend has it that in 1465, King Kazimierz IV fed Cabbage Rolls to his army prior to the battle of Malbork against the Teutonic Order. Victory was credited to their high nutritional value and strength-boosting qualities. Well, if they were good enough for the king's men, they're certainly good enough for the rest of us. This dish is on Peter's list of top five Polish dishes ever; he loves them with a dill and butter drenched new potato, a chunk of fresh seeded rye, and a small glass of icy Polish vodka straight from the freezer. Heaven on earth...

YIELDS 18 rolls

2 onions, chopped
1 tablespoon vegetable oil, butter or bacon fat
1 1/2 cups cooked rice
1/2 pound ground beef

1/2 pound ground pork
salt and pepper
1 head of cabbage (approximately 3 pounds)
1 cup of beef broth

Fry the onions in oil, butter or bacon fat until golden. Mix the onions with the rice, beef and pork and season with salt and pepper.

Place the whole head of cabbage in a large pot of boiling water. Cover and cook for 5 minutes. Remove the cabbage from the pot and gently separate a few soft outer leaves from the head. Return the cabbage to the pot and continue to cook for 3 minutes. Remove the cabbage from the pot again and separate a few more softened outer leaves. Repeat this process until all leaves are separated. Cut out the hard center stem from each leaf.

Place about 1/8 cup of the meat mixture, in a small loaf-shaped mound, on each cabbage leaf. Roll the leaf around the stuffing, the long way, folding each side over the stuffing like an envelope, to seal the sides. Place the stuffed cabbage rolls next to each other in a baking dish small enough that the cabbage rolls are tightly packed. Pour the beef broth over the rolls.

Bake uncovered at 450 degrees for 20 minutes and remove from the oven.

TOMATO SAUCE (prepare while cabbage rolls are baking)
1 14 ounce can of plum tomatoes
1/2 cup of butter
salt and pepper

In a sauce pan, bring the tomatoes and butter to a boil. Break up the tomatoes as they cook. Reduce to a simmer and cook the tomato butter mixture until it thickens. This may take 20 to 30 minutes.

Blend mixture on low in a blender or with an immersion blender. Salt and pepper to taste.

(recipe continued at left)

(recipe continued from right)
Pour sauce over the cabbage rolls. Cover the baking dish. Reduce the oven temperature to 350 degrees and bake for 1 hour.

Cabbage rolls taste best when reheated, for 45 minutes in a 400 degree oven.

TIP: *Cabbage Rolls taste best when reheated, for 45 minutes in a 400 degree oven.*

PORK CUTLETS
Kotlety Schabowe

Meat has always been an important part of the Polish diet and pork is among the most popular selections. This classic cutlet is a tasty choice anytime and anywhere in Poland. Quite similar to Viennese Schnitzel, the Polish version is often served with boiled cabbage, dill pickles, Marinated Beet Salad *(page 25)*, or Cucumber Salad *(page 21)*.

SERVES 4

4 thin, boneless, center cut pork chops	1 teaspoon marjoram, finely chopped
3 tablespoons flour	salt and pepper
1 egg beaten	2 tablespoons olive oil
1/2 cup bread crumbs	

Trim excess fat from pork chops. Pound the meat to tenderize until about 1/4 inch thick. Cutlets may be cut into smaller pieces to better fit your skillet. Season with salt and pepper.

(recipe continued at right)

(recipe continued from left)
Mix bread crumbs and marjoram.

Dredge the cutlets in flour. Dip in the beaten egg. Roll in bread crumb mixture and press in to make bread crumbs stick to the cutlets.

Fry cutlets in oil until golden on both sides and until the pork is no longer pink – about 5 to 7 minutes per side.

BEETS WITH HORSERADISH
Ćwikła

This is a very classic, truly unique Polish garnish that amazes everyone who tastes it. It is so very easy to prepare and goes well with anything you'd like to enhance with a little extra zest. Whether you're serving kielbasa or ham or a pork cutlet, the added kick definitely takes the flavors up a notch…in a very Polish way. You can make it as strong or mild as your taste buds allow. You can serve it in several strengths to satisfy the palate of everyone sitting at the table. Preparation takes only a couple of minutes – chop, mix, taste, and it's ready to serve. Want a tip to make it even better? Let it sit for a few days. The flavors get richer with time as the horseradish infuses more thoroughly with the beets. Laura and Peter always have a jar in the refrigerator since it stores well for a long time.

YIELDS 2 cups

2 14 1/2 ounce cans of red beets, drained
    and coarsely chopped
5 ounces prepared horseradish
2 teaspoons sugar

Combine beets, horseradish and sugar. Place in a tightly sealed jar and refrigerate.

Note: *More horseradish may be added at any time to satisfy an adventuresome palate.*

FLOUNDER WITH ASPARAGUS
Flądra ze Szparagami

Flounder is a flat fish whose shapely fillets lend themselves well to aesthetic plating. Since flounder is readily available, as opposed to traditional pike and carp of many classic Polish recipes, that makes it a practical fish for many of the dishes we prepare today. In this preparation, we marry the delicate and light essence of flounder with the earthy flavors of mushrooms and the bright green crunch of fresh asparagus. Arrange it attractively on a beautiful platter and you will have an elegant dish that is sure to please everyone around the table.

SERVES 4

FISH
2 pounds flounder fillets
1/4 pound mushrooms, sliced
1 cup vegetable broth
1 tablespoon of soft butter
salt

In a skillet, sauté the mushrooms in 1 tablespoon of butter. Sprinkle fish with salt. Place the fish over the mushrooms. Add 1 cup vegetable broth, cover and simmer for 10 minutes. Flounder cooks very quickly so be vigilant about not letting it dry out. When done, transfer the fish to a warmed serving platter.

SAUCE
1 cup vegetable broth
2 cups vegetable broth, divided
2 tablespoons butter
1 1/2 teaspoons flour
1 teaspoon lemon juice
2 egg yolks
1 tablespoon water
1 pound asparagus
1 tablespoon parsley, chopped

Melt butter in a sauce pan over low heat and blend in flour to make a paste. Gradually stir in the remaining cup of broth to the mixture, stirring constantly until thickened and smooth. Remove the mushrooms and add to the sauce. Remove sauce from the heat. Season with salt and lemon juice. Mix the egg yolks with water and add to the sauce. Place asparagus around the fish. Pour the sauce on and sprinkle with parsley.

Goes well with rice or noodles.

TIP: *Timing is important with this and other fish recipes. To keep the fish fresh and moist when served, Laura suggests that you prep your ingredients for the sauce before putting the fish into the oven. Finish the sauce while the fish is simmering, and assemble your platter just before serving.*

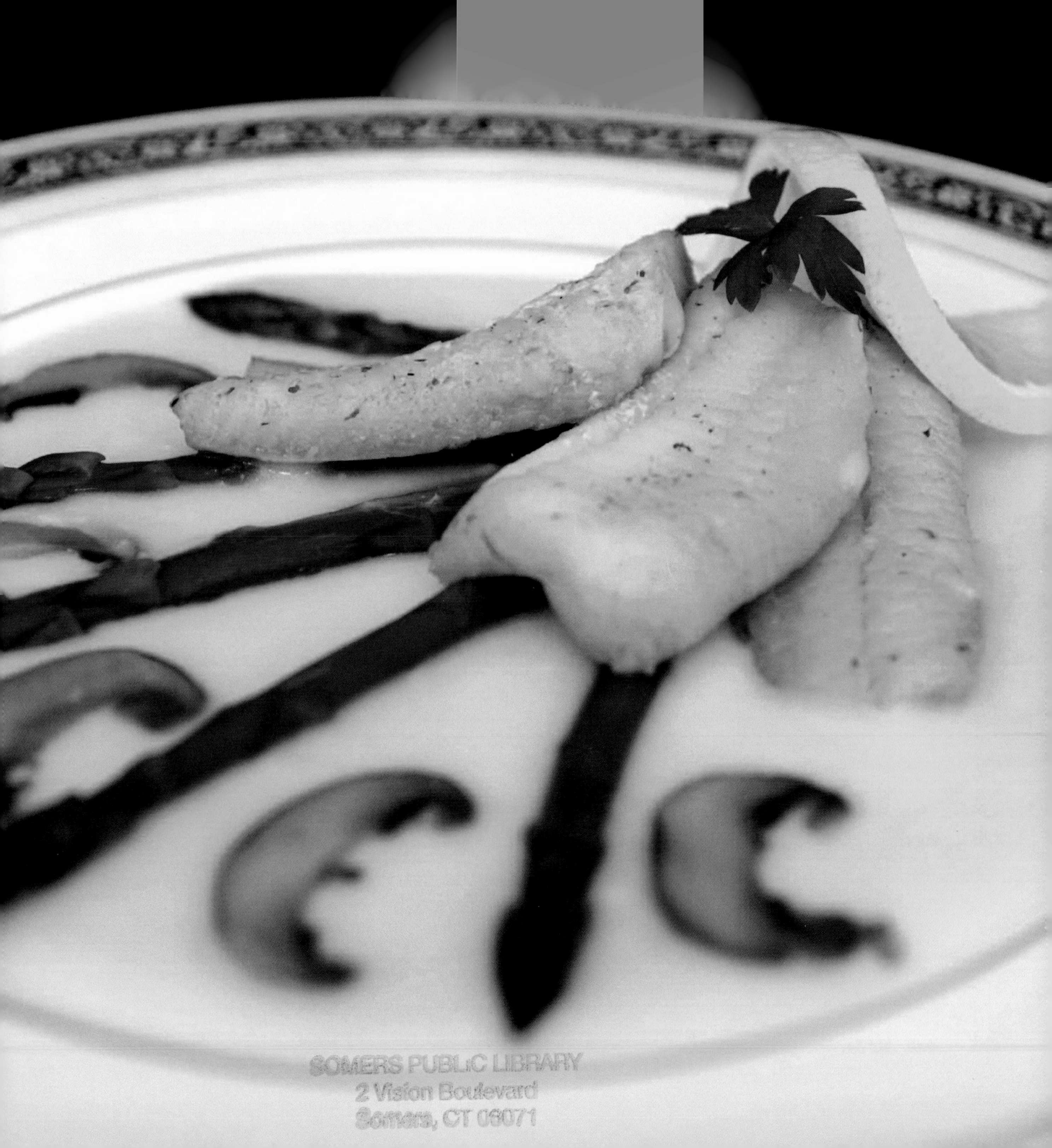

Beef Rolls
Zrazy Zawijane

This dish traces its heritage to medieval times. The Polish name of this dish specifies the traditional Polish cooking technique of pounding thin slices of beef steak, hiding a delicious stuffing in the rolls, and braising them to fork-tenderness. This classic recipe is destined for your private collection of signature dishes, brought out for those truly special meals when you really want to impress. There are several regional variations for the stuffing that use sauerkraut or cheese or even seafood. We like this classic version because the crunchy tang of the dill pickle strips goes beautifully with the flavors of beef and mushroom. Dark rice or buckwheat groats, Vegetables Polonaise *(page 65)*, and a hearty dry red wine provide a memorable meal.

SERVES 4

8 thin slices lean beef steak, 8 inches long by 4 inches wide, about 4 ounces each
8 strips thin bacon, partially cooked
1 dill pickle, cut in pieces lengthwise
1 large onion, thinly sliced
1 1/2 cups dried mushrooms
2 cups beef stock
1/4 cup flour, seasoned with salt and pepper
1/2 cup water
1/2 cup sour cream
2 tablespoons cooking oil
2 tablespoons butter
1 tablespoon cornstarch

Pre-heat oven to 350 degrees.

Soak the dried mushrooms in warm water for 10 to 15 minutes, then rinse thoroughly to remove any sand. Bring the beef stock to a simmer and add the mushrooms. Remove from heat and let mushrooms soak in the hot stock for at least 20 minutes more.

Place the steak strips between 2 pieces of plastic wrap or wax paper and pound the meat down to about 1/4 inch thickness.

On top of each steak strip place a few onion pieces and a long piece of pickle. Wrap the meat around the pickle and onion and secure with a toothpick or tie with kitchen twine. Repeat with the remaining pieces of steak.

Dredge the beef rolls in the seasoned flour. Wrap each roll with a strip of bacon that has been cooked partially but is still pliable.

Heat 1 tablespoon each of the butter and oil in a skillet on medium-high heat. Add the rest of the onion slices and sauté until browned well. Remove onions from skillet and set aside.

Place the remaining 1 tablespoon of oil and butter in the skillet. Add the beef rolls and brown uniformly on all sides. Place the browned beef rolls in a casserole dish.

Strain the mushrooms from the broth, reserving the broth. Chop the mushrooms
(recipe continued at left)

(recipe continued from right)
and place around the beef rolls in the casserole dish. Distribute the cooked onions on top of the rolls. Pour the broth into casserole dish. Cover the casserole, place it in the oven and bake for 2 hours or until the beef rolls are fork tender.

Remove the beef rolls from the casserole to a serving platter and keep warm. Pour the remaining broth and pan juices into a sauce pan with 1/2 cup water and 1 tablespoon of cornstarch. Bring to a boil. Remove from the heat and wisk in the sour cream. Pour sauce over the beef rolls.

TIP: *Beef round or lean sirloin steak taste best; thin "sandwich slices" are often available in the meat case of better grocery stores. If you choose to slice your own, use a very sharp or electric knife on meat that is very cold and firm, or even partially frozen.*

VEAL STEW WITH DILL
Potrawka Cielęca z Koprem

This is actually a rather delicate dish with amazing flavor. By nature, veal is less rich than mature beef so the lighter approach of adding only celery, onion, chicken stock, and sour cream complements the meat especially well, allowing its flavors to shine. The use of dill, which Laura and Peter believe should be absolutely honored as the "Official Herb of Polish Cooking," makes this stew unique among other cuisines' variations of this dish.

SERVES 4 to 6

2 pounds veal shoulder, cut in 1 inch cubes
2 carrots, thinly sliced
2 celery stalks, thinly sliced
1 onion, chopped
1/4 cup seasoned flour
2 tablespoon olive oil
2 tablespoon butter
3 cups low salt chicken or veal stock
3/4 cup cold water
3 tablespoons flour
2 1/2 tablespoons fresh dill, chopped
salt and pepper to taste
1/2 cup sour cream
additional sour cream and dill for topping

Sauté vegetables in olive oil for 7 to 10 minutes or until tender. Remove to a bowl and set aside.

Dredge veal cubes in seasoned flour and shake off excess. Sauté meat in olive oil and butter until browned.

Add broth and bring to a simmer. Cover and simmer for 20 minutes or until just tender. Add the reserved vegetables and simmer another 10 minutes or until both meat and vegetables are tender.

Mix flour with cold water and gradually stir into the meat and vegetables, to thicken the sauce. Bring to a boil stirring constantly. When the sauce has thickened, add the dill and remove the pan from the heat. Season with salt and pepper. Stir in the sour cream.

Serve over noodles or rice. Garnish each plate with a dollop of sour cream and top the stew with a sprinkle of dill. Serve with Yeast Fingers *(page 14)*, if you have any left over in the freezer.

Sausage and Cabbage
Kiełbasa z Kapustą

Here is a one-pot meal that is both delicious and easy to prepare. The dish brings together two mainstays of Polish cuisine on one plate. The marriage of soft, buttery cabbage with crunchy sausage creates flavors and texture that go extremely well together. The caraway adds a tang which is definitely Polish.

SERVES 6 to 8

1 1/2 pounds cabbage, coarsely chopped
1 large onion sliced
1 tablespoon butter
5 small new potatoes, quartered
1 teaspoon salt
1 teaspoon caraway seed
1 1/2 pounds fully cooked Polish sausage, sliced in 1 inch pieces
1 1/2 cups chicken broth, divided
1 teaspoon cornstarch
1/4 teaspoon sugar
1/2 tablespoon lemon juice

In a large pot, sauté the onions and sausage in the butter until the onions start to brown. Add the cabbage, stir, cover pot and continue to cook until cabbage becomes limp.

Add the potatoes and 1 cup of the chicken broth. Bring to a boil, cover and simmer until the potatoes are tender. To the remaining chicken broth, mix in the cornstarch, sugar, and lemon juice. Add this liquid to the pot. Bring back to a boil and continue to cook uncovered until the sauce thickens slightly. Season with salt and more caraway seeds to taste.

BAKED FISH WITH MUSHROOMS AND CHEESE
Ryba Zapiekana z Grzybami i Serem

Pike and carp are two types of fish commonly found in traditional Polish fish recipes because of their availability in the Baltic Sea. However, any firm, white fish fillets will work well, including cod, haddock, tilapia, sea bass, thicker flounder, and catfish. Sole, though, is not recommended because it's usually sold very thin.

SERVES 4 to 6

2 pounds white fish fillets
3 tablespoons melted butter, divided
1/2 pound mushrooms, thinly sliced
2 onions, sliced
1/2 cup sour cream
5 tablespoons grated cheese
3 tablespoon bread crumbs
salt and pepper

Preheat oven to 350 degrees.

Sauté the onions in 2 tablespoons of butter until lightly browned. Add the mushrooms and continue to sauté until tender. Place the onions and mushrooms in the bottom of a casserole dish. Arrange the fish over the mix. Season with salt and pepper. Spread the sour cream over the fish and sprinkle with cheese. Mix the bread crumbs with 1 tablespoon of butter. Sprinkle the bread crumb mixture over the fish.

Bake for 20 minutes or until fish is flaky and the bread crumbs are browned.

TIP: *Keep in mind that thin fillets cook very quickly, and they will continue to cook in the hot dish before serving. Avoid drying out your fish by not keeping it in the oven longer than absolutely needed. Laura tests doneness by sticking a small fork into the middle and twisting lightly. If the fish is still translucent or not flaky, it will need a bit more time.*

Any grated cheese you enjoy will work with this recipe; Laura likes to use orange cheddar, for the added flavor and color.

POTATO PANCAKES
Placki Kartoflane

There is considerable debate about where this dish originated. It is found in the traditional cuisines of several nations, including Lithuania, Ukraine, Germany, Hungary, Austria, Russia, and others. Also known as Latkas, these potato pancakes are a very popular Jewish dish. Since so many countries claim potato pancakes as their own, they must be good, and we agree! You can serve them in many different ways, such as with savory sauces like mushroom, or sour cream and onion. Another style is with some smoked cheese melted on top. The traditional style in the Polish Tatra Mountains uses *"Oscypek,"* a popular smoked sheep's cheese.

YIELDS 10 to 12 pancakes

2 pounds potatoes, shredded
1 egg
1/2 teaspoon salt
1/4 teaspoon pepper
1 medium onion, grated
3 tablespoons flour
vegetable oil

In a large skillet, heat oil to about 375 degrees. In a bowl, mix the potatoes, egg, salt, pepper, onion and flour Drop the potato mixture into the skillet and flatten the mix so each pancake is about 1/2 inch high. Fry until golden brown – 5 to 6 minutes on the first side and 3 to 4 minutes on the other side.

TIP: *An electric frying pan works well to keep the heat evenly distributed.*

MUSHROOM SAUCE

2 cups mushrooms, thinly sliced
1 large onion, chopped
3 tablespoons butter
2 tablespoons flour
1 1/2 cups light cream
salt and white pepper

Saute mushrooms and onion in hot butter until onions are golden. Sprinkle flour over the mushroom and onion mixture, stirring. Continue to cook stirring constantly until the flour is incorporated. Gradually stir in the cream. Simmer until sauce is thickened. Season with salt and white pepper to taste.

SOUR CREAM AND ONION SAUCE

2 cups sour cream
2 tablespoons finely grated onion
salt and pepper

Mix sour cream and onion. Season with salt and pepper to taste.

NOODLES WITH POPPY SEEDS
Kluski z Makiem

Poppy seeds have been a classic addition to buttered egg noodles, fruit salad dressings, and fragrant yeast breads dating back to the Greeks in the second century, adding a nutty flavor and texture to many dishes. This version has been a very traditional Polish Christmas delicacy for many generations. If you've never tried this dish before, be prepared for a real sensory awakening. The texture of the poppy seeds, with the soft, plump raisins, and sweetness from a bit of golden honey, will make this a favorite of your whole family.

SERVES 4

1/2 pound egg noodles, cooked
1 cup boiling water
3 tablespoons poppy seeds
2 tablespoons honey
1/2 teaspoon vanilla
2 tablespoons melted butter
1 cup raisins

Place the poppy seeds in a bowl and cover with boiling water. Soak for 3 hours. Drain the poppy seeds through a cheese cloth-lined strainer. The poppy seeds soak up water like a sponge, so let them drain in the strainer for several hours. Spread the poppy seeds over a piece of cheese cloth and continue to extract as much water as possible. Place the poppy seeds in a skillet and heat over low heat. Add the honey and vanilla and mash the mixture with a wooden spoon to make a thick paste.

Toss the noodles with the poppy seed paste and mix with butter and raisins.

Vegetables Polonaise
Jarzyny po Polsku

A very simple, delicious, and uniquely Polish way to make your vegetables look and taste more elegant. Whether you are planning to serve one vegetable at the meal or several, this little preparation will change the flavors just enough to make them seem fresh and new.

SERVES 6

1 head cauliflower, or
3 pounds asparagus, or
1 1/2 pounds green or yellow beans, or
1 1/2 pounds brussel sprouts, or
1 1/2 pounds carrots
2 tablespoons butter or margarine
2 tablespoons toasted bread crumbs

Boil salted water in a pot large enough to cover the vegetable. Cover and cook until just tender. Do not over cook.

Drain the vegetable thoroughly.

While the vegetable is cooking, in a saucepan melt the butter on low heat. Add the breadcrumbs and sauté, stirring constantly, until golden brown. Crumb mixture should be dry and not wet.

Place vegetable on a serving platter or bowl and top with the crumb mixture.

TIP: An array of several brightly colored vegetables cooked separately and arranged on an elegant platter makes a lovely dinner party presentation.

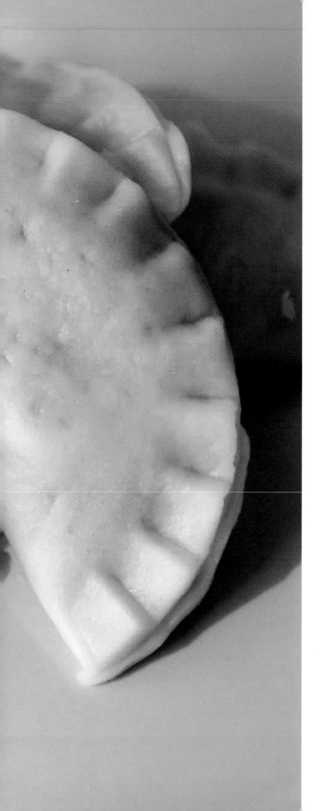

PIEROGI

To the uninitiated, pierogi are filled dumplings, not unlike Italian ravioli. The difference is in the fillings and flavorings. Pierogi can be served as appetizers or entrées, filled with savories such as sauerkraut, cheese, mashed potato, kielbasa, and mushrooms. They can also be served for dessert, filled with fruit preserves, sweet cheese, and topped with a tasty sauce.

Frozen pierogi can be found in the freezer case of your grocery store, or they are often sold unfrozen in Polish or Russian delis; however, these are often mass-produced and don't have the same freshness and intensity of flavors as those you make from scratch at home.

PIEROGI DAY – YUM! After weeks of testing dough recipes and perfecting fillings, it was time for the final exam. This was the last big push to finalize the techniques and taste the fillings. The next day, Laura and Peter's daughter and son-in-law were coming over for a Sunday dinner pierogi-fest. The plan was to serve samples of each variety offered here – seven types of love-filled pockets, complemented by small bowls of sour cream, lightly caramelized onion slivers, and bits of crumbled bacon, as well as sweet toppings to drizzle over the desserts. And, of course, a festive beverage!

The testing took over twelve hours! Laura made over one hundred pierogi. Along the way, she went through eight pounds of flour, a bag of sugar, butter, almost three dozen eggs, cheese, onions, potatoes, sauerkraut, kielbasa, mushrooms, cherries, flavorings and more. By the time the evening news was over on TV, their kitchen looked like a white storm had paused directly overhead. There was flour everywhere – on the counters, on the floor, and all over them. The sink held a mountain of cutting boards, cookie cutters, dough molds, mixing bowls, cooking pots, a pasta maker, rolling pins, and more. Guess who got that assignment!

All day, Peter had a vivid scene in his mind of a kitchen in Poland, decades ago, with Babcia (Polish for "Grandma"), Mama, and maybe a couple of eager youngsters, all working to produce vast platters of pierogi. The experience and skills of previous generations were being passed down – precisely how the traditions and classic dishes of this book survived through the ages.

So what were the lessons learned on that day of pierogi madness? Most importantly, practice will make a big difference. These recipes are great, but executing them properly takes a few tries to get a hands-on feel for the right thickness of the dough, for the right amount of filling in each pierogi, and for the correct cooking times. The result will yield mounds of incredible classic Polish food that everyone will love, and you'll see big smiles from everyone at your table.

PIEROGI DOUGH
Pierogi, Ciasto

YIELDS 45 to 50 three-inch pierogi

2 eggs
2/3 cup milk
1/4 teaspoon salt
2 cups flour
1 egg, beaten with 1 tablespoon of water, for sealing

Whisk together the two eggs, milk and salt. Stir in half of the flour until flour is incorporated, then add the other half and continue to stir. When the mixture comes together to form a thick sticky dough, place the dough on a floured surface. Using additional flour knead the dough until you have a smooth, supple dough that is soft but not sticky. Form the dough into a ball, wrap it in plastic or cover with a bowl and let it rest for 15 minutes.

Take half of the dough and roll it out as thin as possible on a floured surface. It should be almost translucent, approximately 1/8 inch. Cut the dough into 3 or 4 inch rounds or circles.

FILLING

Place a small amount of filling in the center of a dough round. Be sure to leave about a 1/4 inch edge around the entire circumference of your round. Do not use too much filling otherwise the pierogi won't fold in half properly, the filling could spill out or dough will tear. Also, over-stuffed pierogi can burst during cooking. It is better to under fill the pierogi than over fill.

Brush the edges of the circle with the beaten egg. The egg acts as a glue to hold your pierogi together. Fold the dough in half into a half-moon shape. Pinch the edges of the rounds firmly together using your fingers or the tines of a fork. The pinched edges should now appear as one piece of dough. Tight sealing ensures that the edges stay together during cooking. Keep the finished pierogi covered with plastic wrap as you are filling all rounds to prevent the dough from drying.

COOKING

Bring a large pot of well salted water to a boil. In batches, place the pierogi in the boiling water. When the pierogi float or sail to the top of the water, continue to boil for 10-12 minutes. Cooking time will vary according to the size and filling type. Test one to see if the dough is cooked. It should be the texture of moderate to firmly cooked pasta. Remove the pierogi with a slotted spoon and drain.

STORING

For storing and serving later, pierogi may be partially cooked and frozen. Freeze individual pierogi on a covered tray. Try not to stack them against each other. After they have frozen they may be stored in portion-sized plastic freezer bags for up to 6 months.

When ready to serve, remove pierogi from the plastic bags and drop in lightly boiling water. Cook them for just a few minutes until thoroughly heated and the edges are the texture of moderate to firmly cooked pasta.

SAUERKRAUT AND MUSHROOM FILLING

Pierogi z Kapustą i Grzybami

Use same filling as for CREPES on Page 17.

POTATO AND CHEESE FILLING

Pierogi z Ziemniakami i Serem

YIELDS 3 cups

1 pound uncooked potatoes
2 medium onion, finely chopped
2 teaspoons butter
8 ounces cottage cheese, well drained
salt and pepper to taste

Cook the potatoes until fork tender and mash. Do not add any liquid when mashing the potatoes.

Heat the butter in a sauté pan on medium high heat. Add the onions and stir to coat with the butter. Spread the onions out evenly in the pan and cook, stirring occasionally until the onions are soft and caramel colored.

Combine the onions with the potatoes and cottage cheese. Salt and pepper to taste.

Prepare the dough, fill and cook the pierogi *(page 69)*.

Pour a little melted butter over the tops before serving. As another traditional option, melt some butter in a skillet and lightly fry the pierogi on both sides until golden; top with crisp, crumbled bacon and fried onions.

CHEESE FILLING

Pierogi z Serem

YIELDS 1 1/2 cups

1 pound farmers cheese
1 egg
salt and pepper

Combine the cheese and egg, and mix thoroughly.

Prepare dough, fill and cook pierogi *(page 69)*.

To serve, top with a little melted butter. Alternatively, melt some butter in a skillet and fry the pierogi on both sides until golden, and serve topped with crisp, crumbled bacon and fried onions.

FRUIT FILLING
Pierogi z Owocami

YIELDS 2 cups

2 cups fruit: pitted cherries, peeled
  chopped apples, or blueberries
1/2 tablespoon flour
1/2 cup water

1/4 cup sugar
1/4 teaspoon cinnamon
2 to 4 tablespoons fine dry bread crumbs (optional)

Toss the fruit with the flour. Combine the fruit, water and sugar in a saucepan. Over medium heat, bring the fruit mixture to a boil, reduce heat and simmer for approximately 10 minutes until fruit is tender and water is almost evaporated. Remove from heat.

Add cinnamon to fruit and mash slightly. Cook mixture over low heat until thickened, about 5 minutes.

The optional bread crumbs may be added to thickened the fruit mixture further, if necessary,

Prepare dough, fill and cook pierogi *(page 69)*.

SAUCE
1 cup sour cream
1/2 cup confectioner's sugar

Whisk sour cream with the sugar.

To serve as an appetizer, dessert or sweet snack, top the pierogi generously with sauce. Best when warm.

SWEET CHEESE FILLING
Pierogi z Serem Słodkim

YIELDS 1 1/2 cups

FILLING
1 pound farmer cheese
2 1/4 teaspoons vanilla
3 tablespoons sugar
1 egg yolk

Mix the cheese with vanilla, sugar and egg yolk.

Prepare dough, fill and cook pierogi *(page 69)*.

SAUCE
1 cup sour cream
1/2 cup confectioner's sugar

Whisk sour cream with the sugar.

To serve as a dessert or sweet snack, top the pierogi generously with sauce.

LAZY PIEROGI
Leniwe Pierogi

In truth, these are nothing like the other pierogi in this chapter. The intense aromas and flavors of this delicacy are never far from Peter's collection of childhood food memories. Today, so many years later, he can close his eyes and see the kitchen of his childhood…shiny mint-green walls…big white stove with a few black, chipped spots on the white porcelain corners…a big silver-gray pot of boiling water…a long shiny knife…a scuffed, brown cutting board…a log of floured dough being cut into pieces…standing on a wobbly chair to drop them gently in the pot…watching his mother pull them out with a small silver strainer…dusting them with sugar and cinnamon…and finally, the anticipation of wrapping his lips around the first bite. It was a treat to rival all treats. Then and still.

SERVES 4

1 pound farmer's cheese
1 tablespoon soft butter
4 eggs, separated
1 3/4 cups flour
1/2 teaspoon salt

Combine cheese, butter and egg yolks. Beat the egg whites until stiff. Alternating with the beaten egg whites, add the flour and salt to the cheese mixture. Mix lightly. Place dough onto lightly floured board. Form into 3 long rolls approximately 1 inch wide. Flatten the rolls slightly with the blade of the knife. Cut rolls at a slight angle into 2/3 inch pieces. The pierogi will look like small pillows.

Cook in batches in a large pot of boiling salt water. Pierogi will float to the top after about 3 minutes. Continue to cook for another 3 minutes and check for doneness. Surest way is to cut one in half to see if it is cooked all the way through. Cook for an additional few minutes, if needed. Remove from pot with a slotted spoon and drain.

TOPPINGS

Savory: Pour melted butter over pierogi and sprinkle with butter-browned bread crumbs, as in Vegetables Polonaise *(page 65)*.

Sweet: Pour melted butter over pierogi and sprinkle with cinnamon and sugar; or prepare the topping for Sweet Cheese Pierogi *(page 71)*.

TIPS: *The dough will be sticky; before working the dough, lightly flour your hands, cutting board, and knife, to avoid a sticky mess.*

While the pierogi are boiling, the surest way to check for doneness is to simply take one out of the pot, cut it in half and taste – it should be pillowy soft and cooked through the middle, but not chewy like half-cooked pasta.

SWEETS AND PASTRIES

Poles have a sweet tooth, which should be no surprise, and Polish pastries are absolutely on par with any found throughout Europe. The sheer number and variety of cakes, tortes, tarts, cookies, and other baked goods proves that Polish culinary traditions extend way beyond kielbasa, cabbage rolls, and pierogi. On Laura and Peter's last trip to Poland, they were astounded at the number of confectionary shops on so many corners. They could not pass them by. Each was stocked with goodies that were so beautiful, intricate, and just way more than delicious. They gawked and ate their way through two legendary confectionaries which have been going strong since the mid 19th century – Wedel's café on the main square in Krakow, which has been a chocoholic's paradise since 1851, and A. Bikle, whose amazing doughnuts injected with rose hips jam have been favorites in Warsaw since 1869. Their visit to Poland would not have been complete without sampling those classic sweets.

Several of the pastries presented here are traditionally associated with specific holidays – nut rolls, poppy seed rolls, and honey cake for Christmas; mazurkas and baba for Easter. Certainly there are no laws or policies mandating when they can or can't be served. It just seems that generations of families have understood that some of these delicacies stay a bit more special when brought out only once or twice a year, at special times. That's just the way it is and has been for a very long time.

What is especially nice about many Polish baked goods is that they are not so very sweet. Using fresh and natural ingredients such as Italian plums, tart apples, semi-sweet chocolate, cinnamon, and natural honey helps keep these desserts from being too rich or sugary. When it comes to desserts such as plum cake or apple squares, these go well at any time of the year. Plus, these recipes are so versatile that you can take advantage of seasonal produce and change up the flavors at different times of the year.

There are hundreds of recipes for classic Polish sweets. These are Laura and Peter's favorites, and perhaps the favorites of many families, because they are ones handed down so often, and the ones the authors turn to again and again when craving a special ending to a delectable traditional Polish meal.

Plum Cake
Placek ze Śliwkami

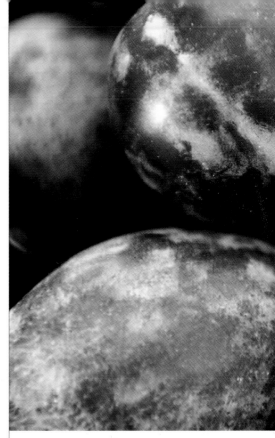

This quick and easy dessert makes great use of an abundance of fresh fruit (plums, nectarines, peaches, apples). In a pinch, it can also be made with canned or frozen fruit. Years ago, these fruit-based cakes were tied to the seasons, with plums being an early fall fruit. But today, when plums are grown all over the world and easily available to most of us on a year-round basis, we are no longer restricted to selected ingredients at specific times of the year. That gives our choice of menus more flexibility, but in a way this bit of progress takes away some of the excitement of anticipating fresh, new flavors as the seasons turn.

SERVES 8

1 cup sugar
1/2 cup unsalted butter
1 cup flour
2 eggs
1 teaspoon baking powder
10 plums, halved and pitted
2 teaspoons sugar
1/2 teaspoon cinnamon
confectioners sugar (optional)

Preheat oven to 350 degrees.

Cream sugar and butter. Add the eggs to mixture and beat well. Add the flour and baking powder and mix until totally incorporated. Put batter into a greased 9-inch spring-form pan sprinkled with bread crumbs. Place the plums cut side down in a circular design on top of the batter. They will sink slightly.

Mix the sugar and cinnamon and sprinkle lightly over the batter.

Bake for 50 to 60 minutes or until a toothpick inserted in the center comes out clean.

Cut into serving portions and sprinkle with confectioner's sugar just before serving.

APPLE SQUARES
Szarlotka

These apple squares are to Poles as apple pie is to Americans. There are as many variations as there are Polish bakers, and while they all passionately debate the merits of their favorites – a little less of this or a little more of that – they pretty much agree that the flavors are more true to their roots when tart cooking apples are used. Another difference from American apple pie is that the crust may be a little sweeter because it relies on butter. Apple squares are a classic found on many Polish restaurant menus and in most confectionary shops.

YIELDS 32 squares

DOUGH

1/2 cup butter	1 egg yolk
4 cups flour	1/3 cup sour cream
1 cup confectioners sugar	grated rind from 1 lemon
2 eggs	

Cut the butter into the flour using a knife and rub the butter in with your fingertips. Or, use a standing mixer on low speed and mix until dough resembles course crumbs. Add the sugar and mix. Mix in the eggs, egg yolk and sour cream. Knead the dough until it leaves the sides of the bowl and forms a ball.

Divide the dough in half and on a lightly floured surface, roll out two 8 1/2 x 12 inch rectangles. Place one in a buttered 9 x 12 pan lined with parchment paper. Bake in a 375 degree oven for 15 minutes.

Remove from oven and cover with apple filling. Cover with the second rectangle. Return to the oven and bake an additional 45 minutes.

Cool slightly. Sprinkle with confectioners sugar to serve.

FILLING

4 1/2 pounds Granny Smith apples, peeled and sliced	1 1/2 teaspoon cinnamon
3/4 cup sugar	1 1/2 teaspoon vanilla

Combine apples with sugar and simmer on low heat until apples are tender. Add the cinnamon and vanilla to the cooked apples.

TIPS: *For a more rustic appearance, the second rectangle of dough may be cut into 1-inch wide strips and layered on top of the apples in a lattice pattern.*

To add another layer of flavoring, a few tablespoons of raisins or candied orange rind may be added to the filling mix.

Chocolate Mazurka
Mazurek Czekoladowy

Mazurek is a very special type of cake traditionally baked in Poland for Easter. The bottom or base is like a shortbread – quite thin because the dough is not meant to rise. It is somewhat crumbly and most definitely delicious. It is usually decorated with nuts or marzipan in artistic designs, such as a pussy willow branch signifying a celebration of spring, or inscribed with *"Wesolego Alleluja,"* a traditional Polish greeting for "Happy Easter." It is speculated that this cake was inspired by sweet Turkish desserts, but its origin is not clear. No matter – Poles have embraced the mazurkas into their own traditional cuisine. It looks good and it tastes good, so it must be good, regardless of where it came from ages ago.

YIELDS 48 pieces

DOUGH

2/3 cup soft butter	1 egg
2 3/4 cups sifted flour	1 egg yolk
2/3 cup confectioners sugar	1/4 cup sour cream
2 teaspoons baking powder	

Cut the butter into the flour using a knife. Then rub the butter in with your fingertips until dough resembles course crumbs. Or, use a standing mix on low speed, and mix until dough resembles course crumbs. Add sugar and baking powder and mix. Add the remaining ingredients. Knead the dough until it leaves the sides of the bowl and forms a ball. Refrigerate in a covered dish for 30 minutes.

Remove dough from refrigerator and roll into a 12x15 rectangle. Place in a 12x15 pan. Spread the dough until the pan is covered. Bake in a 375 degree oven for 20 minutes. Remove from the oven and let cool slightly while you prepare the topping.

TOPPING

12 ounces semi-sweet chocolate	1 1/4 cups sugar
1/3 cup coffee cream	1 tablespoon flour
4 egg yolks	2 tablespoons chopped almonds
1 teaspoon vanilla	

Melt the chocolate with the cream in the microwave or in a double boiler. Beat the egg yolks with sugar until fluffy. Add the flour. Mix the melted chocolate with the egg mixture. Stir in the almonds.

Spread the chocolate mixture over the slightly cooled dough. Bake in a 300 degree oven for an additional 10 minutes.

Remove from oven and cool. Cut into small 2-inch squares or triangles.

POPPY SEED ROLLS
Strucle z Makiem

In Peter's family, this delectable dessert was always served around the holidays. It's very traditional and goes back many generations. If you've tried this delicacy then your mouth should be watering right now. And if not, just close your eyes for a moment and picture yourself sitting before a platter over which hover little whiffs of vanilla, fresh honey, plump raisins, walnuts and almonds, orange and lemon, and just above it all the fragrance of a fresh, yeasty dough just out of the oven. Now gently wave your hand to pull these aromas toward your nose and breathe in deeply. That combination is mysterious, alluring, and intoxicating. Is your mouth watering yet? Okay, open your eyes now and resolve to bake a batch of poppy seed rolls right away! It doesn't matter what time of the year it is. You won't be sorry.

YIELDS 4 rolls

DOUGH

3/4 cups butter	2 egg yolks	2 tablespoons dry active yeast
5 cups flour	1/2 cup sour cream	1/4 cup warm water
1 cup confectioners' sugar	1 teaspoon vanilla	1 tablespoon sugar
2 eggs	1 tablespoon grated lemon rind	

To prepare by hand: In a large mixing bowl, combine the flour with the butter. Cut the butter into the flour with a knife or pastry cutter and then rub in with fingertips. Add confectioners' sugar with the butter and flour. Mix the yeast with 1/4 cup of warm water and sugar. Add the rest of the ingredients including the yeast mixed with the sugar. Turn the dough out on to a lightly floured surface knead the dough with your hands for about 8-10 minutes until the dough is smooth and elastic.

TIP: *Dough may also be prepared using a mixer with a dough hook for kneading. Kneading time will be approximately 5-8 minutes.*

FILLING

1 pound poppy seeds	1 egg, beaten	1/4 cup chopped walnuts
1 cup sugar	1/2 cup honey	1/4 cup chopped almonds
1 teaspoon vanilla	1/4 cup candied orange rind	1/2 cup golden raisins
8 tablespoons butter	1 teaspoon grated lemon rind	2 egg whites

Simmer the poppy seeds in a pot of water (enough to cover) until soft, about 40 minutes. Stir frequently. Drain the poppy seeds using a fine sieve. Press as much water as you can from the seeds. Place the seeds in a bowl and set aside for a couple of hours or overnight to allow excess moisture to evaporate. Grind the poppy seeds in a food processor for about 4 minutes. Add the walnuts and almonds to the poppy seeds and grind for a few seconds. Melt the butter in a saucepan or skillet. Add the poppy seed mixture, sugar, raisins, vanilla, honey, orange peel and lemon rind, and cook over medium low heat for 10 minutes. Cool slightly and add the beaten egg. Whip the egg

(recipe continued at left)

(recipe continued from right)
whites until stiff peaks form and fold into the poppy seed mixture. Let cool.

Divide the dough into 4 equal parts. Roll each piece into a rectangle. Spread each rectangle with an equal amount of filling leaving a one inch margin from each edge. Starting on the long end, roll the dough into a log and seal the ends.

With the seam side down, place the rolls on a non-stick or a greased cookie sheet.

Place the rolls in a warm oven to rise. Let stand until the rolls double in size – about 1 hour.

Bake at 350 degrees for 30 minutes. Let them cool.

ICING

2 cups confectioners' sugar
1/3 cup lemon juice, or rum

Mix the confectioners' sugar and lemon juice. Spread on the rolls and decorate with candied orange rind.

HOLIDAY NUT ROLLS
Strucle z Orzechami

For many Poles who prepare *"Wigilia"* (Christmas Eve dinner), nut rolls are a beloved part of the dessert tray for this traditional feast. Laura has been working with this recipe for almost 40 years, and it reflects all the updates and improvements made after baking over 200 of these delicious baked goods. They also make very popular holiday gifts for friends and neighbors.

YIELDS 5 nut rolls

DOUGH

5 cups flour	1 cup milk divided
1/2 cup sugar	2 ounces yeast or 1/4 cup
1 pound butter	1 tablespoon vinegar
4 egg yolks (save the whites)	

To prepare by hand: in a large mixing bowl, combine the flour with the sugar. Cut the butter into the flour with a knife or pastry cutter and then rub in with fingertips. Add the egg yolks mixed with 1/2 cup of cold milk. Mix the yeast with 1/2 cup of warm milk and mix into the dough. Knead the dough with your hands. Add the vinegar and continue to knead the dough until it pulls away from the sides of the bowl. Form a ball, cover and refrigerate overnight.

TIP: This dough will not rise.

Dough may also be prepared using a mixer with a dough hook for kneading.

FILLING

4 egg whites (saved from dough)
1 cup sugar
2 teaspoons lemon juice
1 pound of walnuts, chopped medium

Beat the egg whites with a mixer until they form stiff peaks. Beating constantly, add the sugar one spoonful at a time. Add the lemon juice and beat 1 minute more. Add the walnuts and fold into the egg white mixture until nuts are evenly distributed.

Cut the dough into 5 equal pieces. Roll each piece into a rectangle. Spread each rectangle with an equal amount of stuffing leaving a one inch margin from each edge. Starting on the long end roll the dough into a log and seal the ends.

With the seam side down place the rolls on a non-stick or a greased cookie sheet. Brush each roll with egg white. Bake in 350° oven for 35 to 40 minutes. Turn pans half-way through baking to ensure even browning.

For the Christmas holidays, rolls may be drizzled with your favorite glaze, sprinkled with crushed nuts and decorated with red and green cherries.

TIPS: You may want to better your skill with this recipe by first practicing the rolling of the dough. Dividing the ball of dough into 8 to 10 equal but smaller pieces (instead of 5) will yield more rolls but the baking time will need to be shorter. Whether doing 5 rolls or 10, the dough should be rolled out to about 1/4- to 1/3-inch thickness. Dough that is too thick will be more difficult to roll and will require a longer baking time. If the dough is rolled too thin, the rolls may crack while baking and the bottoms may get too dark or burn. In truth, the author has scraped brown layers off many nut rolls over the past 40 years. Finally, if you have a perforated French bread form, baking the logs in the form will help each roll keep its shape and prevent splitting or cracking of the dough.

WALNUT TORTE
Tort Orzechowy

There are many varieties of Polish tortes, but for Peter, this is the undisputed king of Polish cakes – number one on his list of all-time favorite Polish desserts. Tortes are very different from American-style cakes since they are made mainly with egg whites, sugar, and ground nuts rather than flour. The icing for this torte is based on eggs and butter, rather than butter and cream. A splash of vodka provides the liquid rather than cream. A dozen eggs go into this torte! When Laura bakes this cake, she and Peter often have a heated discussion about how much vodka to use. She wins if the torte is being baked for company, but if it's for Peter's birthday, his heavier hand prevails.

SERVES 16

BATTER

8 eggs, separated
2 cups confectioners sugar
juice of 1 lemon
8 ounces walnuts, ground
1 teaspoon vanilla

Beat the egg yolks with the sugar for 4 minutes. Add the lemon juice. Beat the egg whites in a separate bowl until stiff. Alternating in small portions, fold the walnuts, egg whites, bread crumbs and vanilla into the egg and sugar mixture. Mix slightly.

Divide the batter between three 9-inch round cake pans that have been buttered and lined with wax paper. Bake in a 350 degree oven for 30 minutes. Remove from oven and cool in pan.

ICING

4 egg yolks
11/2 cups confectioners sugar
1 cup unsalted butter
1 teaspoon vanilla
2 tablespoons instant coffee
1 teaspoon cocoa
2 tablespoons vodka

Cream the butter. In a separate bowl, beat the egg yolks with the sugar. Combine with the butter. Add vanilla extract.

Dissolve instant coffee and cocoa in the vodka. Mix with the cream icing gradually.

Spread icing between the layers, on the top and all around sides of the torte. Decorate with additional crushed nuts, slices of maraschino cherry, or dried fruit pieces if desired.

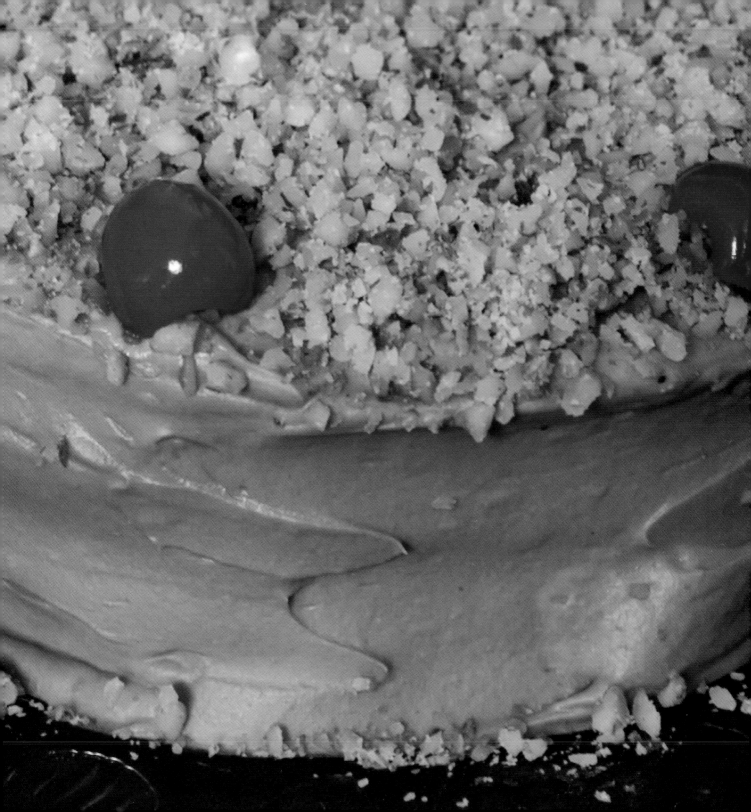

ANGEL WING CRISPS
Chruściki

These light, fried cookies are a favorite for special occasions such as Christmas Eve, Easter, or other celebrations. They are quite elegant, making them a perfect addition to your list of holiday treats. The dough itself is not sweet; most of the sweetness comes from the powdered sugar sprinkled on just before serving. These cookies are very light and fragile because of the kneading process which injects air into the dough. Pile them high and watch them disappear.

YIELDS 7 to 8 dozen

6 egg yolks	1 teaspoon lemon zest
1 whole egg	1 teaspoon orange zest
3 tablespoons sugar	2 1/4 cups flour
3 tablespoons sour cream	1/4 teaspoon baking powder
2 teaspoon light rum	1/2 teaspoon salt
1 teaspoon vanilla	3/4 cup vegetable oil for frying
1 teaspoon orange extract	3/4 cup confectioners' sugar
1 teaspoon lemon extract	Additional flour for kneading

Cream the egg yolks and whole egg with the sugar. Add the sour cream, rum, vanilla, orange and lemon extracts and zest and mix until smooth.

Sift the flour, baking powder and salt together. Mix into the egg mixture a little at a time to make stiff dough.

Turn the dough out onto a floured surface. Knead the dough, keeping the dough and your surface well floured as you knead. Allow the dough to absorb as much flour as it can until it is no longer sticky.

Separate the dough into smaller portions and roll out very thin. The dough should be almost transparent.

Cut the dough into strips approximately 1 1/2 inches wide and 4 inches long. Make a one inch slit, lengthwise, toward one end of the strip. Pull the long end of the strip through the slit.

Heat the oil to 375 degrees. Fry cookies in small batches in the hot oil turning once. The cookies will fry quickly in a minute or less. They should be evenly golden, not brown.

Drain on paper towels or brown paper. When cool, dust with powdered sugar.

Cookies are best when eaten right away. However, they may be stored in air tight containers with wax paper between layers, without any powdered sugar. Dust them with powdered sugar just before serving.

TIPS: *If you have a deep fryer, the cookies may crisp up more evenly because the oil will hold its temperature more consistently. Also, using a standing mixer with a dough hook works just as well as hand kneading and is considerably easier.*

Honey Cake from Warsaw
Piernik Warszawski

This is actually a type of ginger cake often baked for the Christmas season. Peter's mother often talked about her family tradition, during her childhood in Warsaw, of going from house to house on Christmas Day to visit close friends and make their Christmas greetings. Each hostess tried to outdo the others with her variety of baked goods displayed elegantly on the buffet table. Honey cake was found in every home because it is so traditional. This recipe is a favorite of Peter and Laura's family, who delight in the spiciness of the cake, the sweet jam spread between the layers, and the not-too-sweet chocolate icing on top – the more the better.

YIELDS 32 pieces

BATTER

1 cup sugar	1 teaspoon allspice
3 tablespoons boiling water	1 1/2 teaspoon cinnamon
2 tablespoons butter	1 teaspoon cloves
1 cup honey	1 teaspoon grated orange rind
1 cup sour cream	1 teaspoon baking powder
4 egg yolks	4 cups flour, sifted

Brown 1 tablespoon sugar in a saucepan. Add 3 tablespoons boiling water and stir until sugar is dissolved. Add the remaining sugar, butter and honey. Bring mixture to a boil. Remove from heat. Add sour cream, egg yolks, spices and orange rind. Mix well. Add the soda and flour. Beat for a few minutes. Sprinkle the bottom of a buttered 9x12 pan with bread crumbs and pour in the mixture. Bake in a 350 degree oven for 45 minutes. Cool. Remove cake from pan. Cut the cake into 2 layers using a sharp, long-blade knife.

SPREAD

2 cups seedless raspberry jam

Spread the jam over the bottom cake layer. Cover with the top layer. Set cake aside while you prepare icing.

ICING

12 ounces semi-sweet chocolate
4 tablespoons butter
1/2 cup coffee cream, hot

Melt the chocolate and the butter in the cream over low heat. DO NOT BOIL. Spread over the top of the cake and let it firm up.

To serve the cake, cut into pieces about 1 inch wide x 3 inches long. Store tightly covered. This cake is best when served the day after it is made.

BABA WITH RAISINS
Babka z Rodzynkami

It is quite possible that 400 years ago this cake could have been named after someone's grandmother since that is what the words *"baba"* and *"babka"* mean. When it comes out of a fluted tube pan, its sides may resemble the shape of grandmother's pleated skirt. Traditionally, a Baba is tall, round, rustic, and may be prepared in several varieties. It is quite a simple cake, even with the golden raisins or other dried fruit mixed into the delicate, yeast-risen dough. This version, often made for Easter, is certainly a classic, having been around over four centuries. Another legend (which Peter likes) is that in the mid 1600s, the Polish King Stanislas Leszczynski had become very tired of eating the cold, hard, dry bread that was served at his meals and started dipping it in spirits. That practice caught on, and with Peter's palate as well. He likes to sprinkle his baba with a little rum "just to kick it up a notch," he says.

SERVES 10 to 12

1/2 cup soft butter	4 cups flour
1/2 cup sugar	1 cup scalded milk, cooled
3/4 teaspoons salt	1 cup golden raisins
6 egg yolks	1/2 cup sliced almonds
2 1/4 teaspoons dry yeast	1 egg yolk, beaten
1/4 cup lukewarm water	2 tablespoons water
rind of 1 lemon, grated	fine bread crumbs
1/2 teaspoon cinnamon	

Cream butter and sugar in a large mixing bowl. In another bowl, add salt to the egg yolks and beat until thickened. Add egg mixture to the butter and sugar. Stir yeast into the lukewarm water until dissolved. Add yeast, lemon rind and cinnamon to the butter and sugar mixture. Gradually mix in the flour alternating with the milk. Beat well to make smooth dough. Add the golden raisins and knead the dough by hand, or use a standing mixer with dough hook, until it no longer sticks to your hands.

Cover the dough and let rise in a warm place until doubled in size (1 to 1 1/2 hours).

Butter a fluted tube pan and sprinkle all over with fine bread crumbs. Sprinkle 1/4 cup of almonds in the bottom of the pan. Fill pan half full with dough. Beat the remaining egg yolk with 2 tablespoons of water and brush the top. Sprinkle dough with the remaining one quarter cup of almonds. Let dough the rise in a warm place, such as your oven at no higher than 100 degrees, until dough rises to the top of the pan (about one hour).

Heat your oven to 350 degrees and bake for 30 minutes. Let the Baba cool for 10 to 15 minutes and carefully remove from the pan.

INDEX OF RECIPES

ACKNOWLEDGEMENTS

We are very grateful for all the encouragement and support received from all our friends and family, especially:

Christina and BJ, our daughter and son-in-law, for tasting, feedback, and for allowing us to fill your refrigerator,

Daniel Dalcin, for your inspired food stylings and culinary savvy,

David Lovejoy, for keeping us on a sound legal footing,

Jeanne Stanley, Cheryl Butler, and Jeanine Smith, for letting us into your china closets,

Kit Wohl, for sharing your experience and advice from beginning to end,

Matthew Aron Roth, for your "extreme" photography,

Michael Lauve, for your very creative layouts,

Paul J. Watkins, for helping keep the "grammar police" at bay,

Sallie Stubenhofer, for sharing your family's recipe journal, kept safe by Judith Flak Mahoney, Bebe Kij Flak, and Loraine Domanski.

Left: Matthew Aron Roth, *Food Photographer*
Right: Daniel Dalcin, *Food Stylist*